The Comic Catholic

Ronda Chervin

En Route Books and Media, LLC
Saint Louis, MO

ENROUTE
Make the time

En Route Books and Media, LLC
5705 Rhodes Avenue
St. Louis, MO 63109

Cover credit: Sebastian Mahfood

ISBN-13: 979-8-88870-174-4

Library of Congress Control Number: 2024937852

What's Inside

What's Inside

Foreword

G.K. Chesterton viewed humor as an entrée into the spiritual life, and the reason is a simple one: it's rational. As human persons created in the image and likeness of God as individual substances of a rational nature, we find our rational faculty the very thing that enables joyful communion with our Creator.

After a fashion, Ronda Chervin's purpose in the writing of this book is similar—calling to mind the value of humor as a tool for spiritual growth. She demonstrates in this short tome the importance and power of levity in a world we often take more seriously than our humility, charity, meekness, and liberality should allow.

As a philosopher, Ronda understands that risibility, or the ability to laugh, is a property of the human person, and as a *Catholic* philosopher, she understands it is an important tool to cultivate for comporting oneself in a faith that embraces suffering and in a world that provides many opportunities to do so.

If our personal suffering is best offered up for the benefit of the souls in Purgatory, then we ought to be able to offer it with grace, and a way to do that is to look for the ironies within it, look for the lessons it can teach us, and smile. God loves a cheerful giver.

Certainly, we might say, we can't make a joke out of every tragedy and some things *ought* to be taken seriously. And, sure, that's also true. If virtue, though, is in the mean, then we are permitted to show the right emotions for the right situations to the right people at the right time. And among our options, as we wrestle with our irascible appetite, is to kick our head back and say, "Wow! Good one, God!"

If nothing else, it makes us feel better to think of God as laughing *with* us!

- Dr. Sebastian Mahfood, OP,
author of *The Narrative Spirituality of Dante's Divine Comedy*

Introduction

When I happen to be around non-Catholics, I am somewhat blocked in my enjoyment of telling jokes. The 'others' might not get the Catholic references.

For example:

When I was living temporarily with my best friend, Marti, another Dedicated Catholic Widow, I put some fragrant hand-lotion on my face. Marti looked up and started to sniff appreciatively. She said:

"What's that wonderful smell?"
"It's just my hand-lotion," I replied.
"Oh, I thought it might be the odor of sanctity!"

Would a non-Catholic get that humor? Possibly, but probably not.

I thought my Catholic readers might enjoy a little book full of such Catholic jokes.

"Here goes nothing," as we used to say in New York City when I was a child.

But, first, a few general thoughts about humor.

A Catholic Hollywood comedienne, Mary Mitchell, used to give talks about comedy. One of my favorite lines from these talks was this:

> "At the end of the day, think of the scene you thought was tragic and play it for comedy."

At first hearing that suggestion, it sounded impossible and even cruel. But, take a look at this incident:

A beloved professor of English, known for his sense of humor, was slowly dying at a hospital. Finally, he died, and many came to Memorial Mass. On the way in, we wanted to show our compassion to his beloved wife. To our surprise she told everyone about her husband's final joke:

> "A minute after the hospital called to tell me he had passed away, the toilet seat cracked in two!"

Abraham Low was the psychiatrist founder of Recovery International (not 12 Step), a mental health program for coping with anger, anxiety, and depression. He had the participants in his program say to themselves often throughout the day:

> "Anger is your worst enemy. Humor is your best friend."

Why so? For one, lots of anger comes from wounded pride – 'how dare he/she insult me that way!' But when we laugh, we can see the same insult as kind of funny.

Humor is also a kind of antidote to a syndrome you may not know by its name but probably know when you run into it – it's called angelism. There are human beings with bodies as well as souls who wish they were pure spirits, constantly in the realm of ideas and ideals, instead of having to cope with the daily-life problems of living in a body—such as cooking, working, weather…it's as if a dog spent his/her days longing to be a human! Now laughter at the little problems of daily life is much better than peevish anger!

The great English Catholic writer, G.K. Chesterton, thought that whereas most of us believe in such attributes of God as Just, Merciful, Good, All-Powerful, All-Knowing…he believed, also, in a hidden side of God – His laughter at our human foibles.

When I started writing *The Comic Catholic*, I noticed that there are many different meanings of the word "funny."

Ha - ha – funny: such as in "What's a cat's favorite color in Lent? Purple."

Word - play – funny: such as in puns like "The best way to communicate with a fish is to throw it a line."

Sarcastic – funny: ridiculing, such as in a driver's speeding around someone on the freeway, and another driver yells out "Get the hell out of here."

Sardonic – funny: this is like sarcastic humor but lighter, such as "For some 'progressive' priests the only sin is not hitting other cars in the parking lot."

Anomalies-of-daily-life – funny: such as "Everyone asks 'how are you?', but no one wants to know."

Self-Deprecatory – funny: You have certainly heard this genre of humor but probably without knowing it as a definite type. 'Deprecatory' is a word for disapproving. Being self-deprecatory means talking about one's own faults readily. One psychological reason for this I have heard is that by mentioning a flaw about oneself aloud one doesn't have to hear the same criticism from others. It is already out there. Example: I tell everyone in advance that I am a very angry person. "Watch out, I may just kill you someday."

Unexpected-responses – funny: when leaving people whom I may never see again in this life, instead of saying 'See you soon,' I say "see you in Purgatory!' I realize, as I am observing conversations with this book in mind, that unexpected-response-funny is a huge category…most of my own humor as of this type. So many of my personal examples are not funny in the ha-ha sense at all, but people find them funny in the sense of unexpected.

(Note: *The Comic Catholic* was written while I was living with my friend Marti Armstrong, a Pastoral Counselor and a Dedicated Widow, and another friend, Eileen Busacca, a comedienne, so there are many little jokes from their repertoire.)

(Another note: Some of these stories are not specifically Catholic but people laugh so much when I tell them that I had to put them in!)

Unexpected Happenings and Responses

These accounts are not so much jokes as they are ways of putting things that make people think, but also seem funny in the sense of "odd."

Here are some examples from the Church and some of my own:

> St. Francis called the animals brother and sister. But he called the body 'Brother Ass!'

I think this is so funny because it is unexpected. Most of us think of the body as this part of ourselves which is sometimes wonderful as in eating and swimming and dancing, etc., but also a burden when there is pain or debility of aging. But we don't think of it as Brother Ass.

When Pope Francis was named Pope, he was being dressed in the proper clothing to appear on the balcony at St. Peter's Square. One who does not delight in fancy dress at all, he insisted that he would not wear silky red slippers: "It's not Mardi Gras!"

A healing priest came from far to perform a service for a group at a parish. About 300 people came. He said,

> "If Pope Francis was coming there would be standing room only. But Francis' boss, Jesus, is here tonight.'

Some Sisters ran out of gas on a highway. They didn't have a proper gas container to bring to a gas station off the road, so they used a bed-pan they happened to have in the trunk of their car. While they were filling up the car someone passed and remarked, "That's faith."

At a youth rally where Pope John Paul II could see the young people were restless, he raised his fingers in circles upside down around his eyes and started singing to them instead of preaching.

I was on my way by plane to give a retreat at a remote place. The airplane I needed for the final stage of the trip was delayed. I was telling the man at the counter: "I am giving this Catholic retreat, and I have to get there. Please tell me the plane will arrive soon."

Evidently, the counter man was a Catholic because he looked at me and said, "Why don't you offer it up?"

I was planning a trip to Corpus Christi, Texas, where I have lived three different times. One of my publishers, James Ridley, of Goodbooks Media, hearing I was coming back to Corpus Christi for Christmas wrote me:

> "There are giddy rumors fluttering around the abodes of your abandoned aficionados that you may be migrating back to Corpus Christi. We are gathering palm fronds in case you choose to ride in on a donkey."

In the Bible Belt, some Christians wear crosses but not crucifixes. So, when someone, such as a cashier at a store noticed my crucifix some would say, "I like your necklace."

I would reply: 'Oh, you love Jesus,' and then engage in a dialogue if no one else was in line.

My friends Marti and Eileen walked to daily Mass in a blizzard when no one could drive. The priest was surprised. He said "Why are you here! You don't have to come to daily Mass."

Marti replied: "You don't *have* to eat a hot fudge sundae, but I bet you eat it."

(When I visit anyone who seems near to leaving this world, I ask them what their best advice for me is.)

Tom - Why do you expect irrational people to act rationally?

Ronda: People only seem fulfilled after a delicious meal!

When Catholics leave others saying "have a great day!" I sometimes surprise them by saying:

> "What is a great day for a Christian? One where we get to suffer a lot with Jesus!"

Most funny, in the sense of unexpected, remarks came from my son, Charles…

> "Mom, you think you are a terrible Catholic because you are so angry, but I think you are a wonderful Catholic because you are so vulnerable."

> "Why was Noah the best businessman in the Bible? He floated his stock while everybody else was being liquidated."

> What's the difference between Jesus and your father? Your father never came back.

Marti Armstrong: "Even though my husband, a skier, loved snow, when he saw it the first time each winter he would say:

> "Maybe the angels are shaking their heads!"

A bumper sticker reads: "Do you follow Jesus this closely?"

When Winston Churchill was writing a book, his editor reminded him to "never end a sentence with a preposition." He replied humorously: "This is something up with which we should not put."

My friend, Marti Armstrong, was sending out donations. One was for Food for the Poor. I said "Bravo" commending her for her munificent charity. She replied: "I'm adding a little note to send me back a little money to buy a popsicle."

Belief in God

Apologetics is the name given for defending the Catholic faith. These stories are odd and funny but also good for use in showing non-believers why the Catholic faith is true. Most of the stories in this section are of the type of humor that is not "ha-ha" but that comes as a kind of surprise when there is an unexpected response.

A man who was an atheist noticed an older man praying his rosary in a train in France. He gave him a long talk about how there was no God. At the end of his speech, the old man handed him his business card: Louis Pastcur, M.D.

For many Christians the most difficult question to answer when talking to non-believers is how there can be a God of love when there is so much suffering in the world. I love the reply of Betsy Ten Boom, the famous martyr of the Nazi concentration camps. When asked this question by other prisoners she would say:

"If you know Jesus, you don't have to know why!"

People ask how can I believe in a God of love when there is so much suffering in the world. I like to say if you were tortured every day of your life but had an infinity of joy in heaven, do the math! Wouldn't it be worth it?

Sometimes we wonder how God who is Perfect Being can love little us humans. My joke is that there is an abyss between my nature and my pet cat's nature, but I have no trouble loving her! Even when she bites and scratches, I have no more trouble forgiving her than God has forgiving us our sins.

Graffiti in a New York City Subway Station in the 1960's:

"God is dead." Nietzsche
"Nietzsche's dead." God

When I am very appreciative of the character or the good deeds of someone I often say:

> "You are the 6th proof for the existence of God!" (A reference to St. Thomas Aquinas' famous 5 proofs for God's existence.)

When an atheist said: "I don't believe in God" someone replied: "Well, He believes in you."

Proof of the Resurrection? Mel Gibson's movie *The Passion* tells it all. When you see the not-so-beautiful artistic crosses in Churches but what the torture of crucifixion is really like, how can you imagine that the apostles, who knew what it was, and most of whom fled from it, would risk such an end to their own lives if they hadn't seen the Resurrected Christ?

When my friend and publisher Dr. Sebastian Mahfood, OP, met yet another atheist who loudly proclaimed his disbelief in God – something atheists often do when they meet believers – the Lay Dominican said, "Listen, we're all finite beings. Those of us who believe are simply exercising a greater capacity for engaging in wonder at the beauty of creation."

Marriage and Family Jokes

Nowadays, defense of marriage and the family is vital. We might not even want to think about funny sides to it, but I find that even telling stories that make me look bad as a wife and mother does help listeners with ideas about how to improve their marriage and family.

> "I'm not okay. You're not okay, and that's okay." Marti Armstrong

Teaching about dealing with conflicts in marriage, a charismatic leader used to call marriage "the sandpaper ministry." He meant that the faults of each rub against each other and smooth each other out!

> "I thought he was perfect, and he thought I was perfect until we got married!" Marti Armstrong

A happily married Catholic had a funny way of dealing with small conflicts between him and his wife. For example, if his wife forgot to put his favorite drink on the dining table, he would suddenly call out "Divorce!"

I like to teach that in the honeymoon period each one sees the other as a perfect idol-like person. Then after a few years they become fallen idols. But then after they forgive each other for everything, they see each other as funny little creatures, not to be angry at but to laugh at.

My husband was very warm-blooded, and I am always cold. I liked to say that the dual control electric blanket saved our marriage. He kept his thermostat at 1 and I kept mine at 10!

One of my daughters told me, "We always thought Martin was the only man who ever could have been married to you!" I took it as an insult, but over a long time of widowhood, I have begun to think she was right!

When I became a widow, I would say to married couples – here is what I learned from becoming a widow:

"The absence of annoyance is not joy."

I have bad hand-eye coordination, so it took me three years after getting my driver's license to learn how to change lanes on a freeway. What gave me the courage was that one day I had a long drive that involved crossing over four different freeways in the Los Angeles area. I had a bad argument with my husband just before I started out. I suddenly thought, "Since I want to die anyway, why not risk changing lanes?"

In the 1970's, in some Catholic circles, there was a big emphasis on male headship. The theory was that it was bad for marriage and family when the husband became the second-in-command and the wife took over. We were discussing this matter with others, and my husband, Martin, told the group in front of me that:

"I don't believe in headship, but if your wife is as stupid as mine, you better be the head."

Most of the people were shocked and horrified, but I understood and laughed and laughed. I am very smart at philosophy but terrible at making everyday prudential decisions.

Even with the sadness of divorce, I have noticed in the case of friends of mine that there can be humor. One divorced man, finding himself alone for Thanksgiving, shaped the burger meat into the form of a turkey.

The ultimate bumper sticker: "Let me tell you about my Grandchildren! No one will stop you."

When a mother of adult children gives them unwanted advice, one of them calls such speeches 'mom-i-lies.'

This is about sharings at a weekly husband's marriage seminar. At one session, the leader asked Paulo, who was approaching his 50th wedding anniversary, to tell about how he had managed to stay married to the same woman all these years. Paulo said: "Wella, I'va tried to treat her nicea, spenda da money on her, but besta of all is, I tooka her to Italy for the 25th anniversary!" The leader asked: "Please tell us what you are planning for your wife for your 50th anniversary?" Paulo proudly replied, " I gonna go pick her up."

Eileen Busacca: At a gathering of married people the leader asked, "Has anyone told you that you are beautiful today?" I leaned over to my friend, Marti, and said:

"Does it count to say 'You're a beaut!"?

Teresa Barardi confessed that when her first husband died she suddenly thought: "Who is going to tell me when I have to get new tires on the car?"

My husband was twenty years older than me and critically ill with asthma for most of our marriage. He often thought about what I would do after he left this world. He would joke:

> "You know, Ronda, in India in bygone ages if a man died his wife had to lie on his funeral pyre and be set on fire so she would die with him. That's what you should do."

At the rosary in the funeral home that night before his Mass and burial, I was giving a short talk about his life. At the end I looked down at the coffin and said:

> "Martin wanted me to agree to die on his pyre. Now that I see the coffin in front of me, I'm not sure I want to do it."

Catholic teenage girls used to pray: "St. Anne, St. Anne, hurry up and get me a man."

Jokes about Failure in Efforts to be Holy

Dietrich Von Hildebrand taught that:

> "There is an abyss between an ardent Catholic and a saint!"

Many serious Catholics know that they are sinners but still make a lot of effort to avoid sins, mortal and venial, and work on defects of character. I find that I need to laugh at my failures regarding not sinning, of course, but to ask for lesser defects.

> St. Teresa of Avila taught that we need never be upset at the bad things that happen in life if we realize that God alone is enough. So, I ask myself why am I frantic when my phone or laptop doesn't work?

I was living at a retreat center and tried to volunteer helping the monks fix up rooms for guests. One of them remarked after an hour of trying to work with me: "Why are you doing this if you're only going to do a second-rate job of it?" I was hurt. I went to the Abbot to tell him about this. Here was his funny advice:

> "Ronda, you are a woman, so you want to help...but you are not good at cleaning, so don't help!"

I used to go to Mass at a Church staffed by Filipino nuns. One of them was known for her holiness. I made an appointment to talk to her and told her about how I try so hard, but I am still so awful. Here is her funny advice:

> "Kill the ego."

I told my spiritual director that I had just read the writings of St. Catherine of Siena. "Now you have a big challenge. You have to make me into Catherine of Siena." He replied:

"God already has St. Catherine. Now, he wants St. Ronda."

I was speaking at a Catholic conference. A woman came up to me after my talk and said: "Dr. Ronda, I have been praying for you for twenty years. That's because I went to a talk of yours long ago and I was horrified that you used the word 'hate' so much." It was funny, in the sense of unusual, for anyone to talk to a speaker that way. However, I made it a point after that to explain that New Yorkers like me use that word a lot where more refined people would talk about dislike.

I like to amuse my friends this way: When I happen to transfer some garment of mine to them or they to me I describe it as a relic! My friend, Sebastian Mahfood, laughs and tells me, "Yes, but it's only second-class."

Jewish/Catholic Jokes

I come from a Jewish but atheistic background. I became a Catholic at age 21. (Buy my book *En Route to Eternity*!) As a result, I love stories involving Hebrew-Catholics and any kind of situations where Jews say something that makes Catholics laugh.

An old Jewish man was hit by a bus in New York City. The street where he was hit was right near a Catholic Church. The priest came running out to see if he was a Catholic and needed the last rites. He bent over the man lying on the street and asked, "Are you a Catholic?" No answer. Then he tried, "Do you believe in the Trinity?" No answer. "Do you believe in three persons in one nature?"

The Jewish man opened his eyes and said: "I'm dying and he's asking me riddles!"

At a protest in front of an abortion clinic where most of us prayer warriors were Catholics, a Jewish man came with a big sign saying: "Hitler laughs in hell every time a Jew has an abortion."

Asked by a Jew why he should become a Catholic, the famous Jewish-convert, Charles Rich, coming out of a lower East Side New York push-cart area where my husband had also been born replied: "You get more!"

My mother-in-law was a Jewish woman who came to the United States around the year 1935. She learned to speak English but only read Yiddish. She was upset that her son married a Jewish person, me, who had become Catholic. She couldn't figure out who Jesus even was. So, when visiting us once she looked through a children's book about Jesus and came up with this conclusion:

> "Now, I understand. Jesus was a nice Jewish boy who was kidnapped by the 'Christians.'" (Yiddish word for busy-bodies.)

A priest, a minister, and a rabbi are discussing when life begins. The priests says, “It begins at conception.” The minister says, “Life begins at 24 weeks gestation.” The rabbi says, “You are both wrong. Life begins when the kids move out of the house and the dog dies.”

My husband, a convert from a Jewish background to the Catholic faith, flew across the US to see his sister on her deathbed. His sister was a reformed Jew. He had told her about Jesus and when he reached her bedside he begged her:

> “Why don’t you pray for Jesus, even if you are not sure He is God?”
>
> Her reply was: “Of course. I’m hedging my bets!”

On his deathbed, a Jewish convert to Catholicism was about to make his final confession, and the priest said, “Remember, now is not the time for spiritual direction.”

Jokes about Priests

In our times, perhaps partly due to the scandals involving a tiny minority of them, we want to praise wonderful priests, not joke about them. Just the same, jokes about priests can be very funny.

Fr. Apostoli, the famous priest of the Franciscan Friars of the Renewal, used to tell this one:

> "A priest asked to go to confession to another priest. As a penance, he is told to say a whole Rosary and the Stations of the Cross in between each bead. Then the priest who gave this huge penance asked the first priest to hear his confession. As a penance, he was told: Now you pray the Stations with a whole rosary between each station."

Fr. Benedict Groeschel, the famous founder of the Franciscan Friars of the Renewal, had a freak accident walking in front of a truck in a parking lot. Since he was a speaker on EWTN, thousands of Catholics prayed for him to survive. At his first talk after recovering from this accident everyone in the audience stood up and applauded him. Reaching the podium, he remarked humorously:

> "A stupid old man walks in front of a truck, and he's treated like a martyr."

A Catholic man who didn't believe there should be women priests used to say, "Well, I want to become a nun!"

A cartoon depicts St. Anthony of Padua, patron of lost items, asking God:

> "What did I ever do to deserve an eternity of looking for everyone's car keys."

Working for the Lord don't pay much, but the benefits are out of this world.

Marti Armstrong, my friend, told me this funny incident:

> "I was on the way back from the vet with my dog who was still traumatized by a procedure. So, I brought the dog with me into the living room of a priest when asking for confession. I explained to the priest that the dog would not break the seal of the confessional. The priest was surprised but proceeded with the sacrament. I told about this to another priest. That one had a different opinion: 'Think what he will tell the other dogs!'"

On another subject, some anti-Church writers think of the Catholic Church as a horrible institution where priests get to live in luxury on the donations of the poor. But I say that even in poor countries the Catholic people visit the Church often, not only on Sundays, going in and out on the way from shopping or at the end of the work day.

> "We think of the Church building as our celestial living room. And the priests as our servants."

In the Confessional a man said: "I let my cat drink the bathtub water while I was in it." The priest replied: "Once again, kind of weird but not a sin."

When John Paul II was in New York City, he decided he wanted to get behind the wheel of his limousine and drive in New York City traffic. He asked his chauffeur to sit in the back seat. Well, he missed a red light, and of course the NYPD cruiser came up behind him with the light flashing. The cop approached the driver's door, and the window came down. The Holy Father, seated behind the wheel, realized he didn't have a drivers license. He was about to speak when the cop fainted. When the medic arrived to revive the police officer, the officer sat up and said, "I'm not about to give that guy a ticket! Whoever the guy in the backseat is, he has the Pope for a chauffeur!

At ordinations, there is a part of the ceremony where the priests who know those just ordained walk around to each one and greet them, usually with a handshake or hug of the priest. Everyone in the pews looks on joyfully. I was at an ordination where one of the older priests had been a champion wrestler before feeling called to his religious vocation. When he came up to one of his favorite seminarian "sons" he lifted him up in the air above his own head.

Some daily Mass Catholics imagine that the parish priests have a special fondness for us over the ones who come on Sundays only. One priest had this challenging thing to say: "Oh, we call you Church mice. You are always around giving us unwanted advice!"

My friend, Marti Armstrong calls the cardinals when they fly into her garden, "His Eminence and Her Eminence."

A chef in the kitchen was making chicken and serving it to a Franciscan Priest. They are called friars. He offered him the plate and said: "From the skillet to the Fryer!"

Some of the priest saints were meeting with St. Joseph in heaven. Here is the conversation:

St. Patrick: "Look what they've done to my feast day – the parade has turned into a drunken brawl!"

St. Nicholas: "If you think that's bad, they're celebrating me and not Christ, the son of God!

St. Joseph: "If you think that's bad just think of me. They put me in the ground upside down." (The reference is to a practice of digging a hole in the ground in front of a house one wants to sell and putting in a statue of St. Joseph upside down.)

Conflicts of Daily Life

I struggle with sins of loud anger and irritability, so conflict in daily life is a big category for me. I have been helped by Recovery International for anger, fear, and depression and also by counselors and my own insights that I put in a book *Taming the Lion Within: Five Steps from Anger to Peace*. Incidentally, my friend, Sebastian Mahfood, read that book several years before I met him. When I asked, "Why don't you ever get angry with me?" he replied, "I read your book. Have you?"

When I give talks on dealing with anger, one of the points I make that make people laugh is this:

> "You will be angry every day if your underlying idea of life is 'I am the heroine of the drama of my life…the others are secondary characters there to embellish my happiness or walk-ons.'"

Why? Because your idea for what will make your day good conflicts with their ideas.

From Eileen Busacca:

When an angry driver is giving me the finger for not driving unsafely when he wants me to drive faster, I lower the window and wave and say, "I know your mother, give her my regards."

On a hot day, I was negotiating a place where there were 4 corners each with a light. I didn't want to drive fast just to have to stop at the light, but this other driver wanted me to drive faster and was cursing me and giving me the finger. I called out to him, "Calm down. It's too hot to get that excited. You're gonn'a have a heart attack." The next time he was near he pulled along side of me and apologized and said: "You were right."

Another Catholic said that she was told when anyone gives you the finger raise yours and say, "I'm number one also!"

Moral and Other Controversial Issues

Many Catholics are in agony about some moral and political controversial issues. These stories can add an element of humor that could be welcome.

Alice Von Hildebrand, the famous Catholic woman philosopher taught for years at a non-religious college. When a student would say about abortion: 'It's just a clump of cells," she would reply:

> "So, when your mother is pregnant you are thinking a cat might come out!"

My friend Marti Armstrong, a pro-life leader, puts it this way: "So I'm an adult clump of cells?"

Alice Von Hildebrand again taught that some zealous Catholics, "Could also be pharisaical toward the Pharisees." She was teaching us that you can be as judgmental about them as they are about whoever they consider to be lax.

(To understand this joke, you need to know the distinction between vertical and horizontal inclusive language. Vertical is about God. Horizontal is about the human level as in man and woman for people vs. the word 'man' to cover both sexes.)

A woman who wanted to promote horizontal inclusive language told this joke. "When I passed the men's room on the way into the meeting, I didn't think it included women."

Some Catholics left the Church when they found out that some priests and even bishops were guilty of sexual abuse. My reply is this:

> "When that football coach (Joe Paterno, the Penn State coach) got embroiled in some sexual scandal, no one stopped watching football."

I am a great proponent of living simply so that one has more money to give to the starving. Once, I was invited often for dinner cooked by a priest. Along the wall was a cabinet full of gold rimmed dishes. Since he was a priest devoted to helping the poor, I finally challenged him about this array. He laughed:

> "They're fake gold. I bought the whole set at a bargain store for $20!"

I was teaching ethics at the time of the famous encyclical *Humanae Vitae*. In it, the ban on contraception was defended. Many students didn't know why, especially since at the same time Natural Family Planning was being taught to couples preparing for marriage. Why should pills and devices be wrong, but avoiding pregnancy by a chart be okay?

This unusual analogy seemed to help people understand. Consider that it used to be that black people paid lots of money to straighten their hair. Then came the 'Black is Beautiful' movement. I loved seeing the naturally curly hair in braids on women and men.

Now, I think that a woman shouldn't consider her naturally fertile time to be "my bad time." She should think "Feminine Fertility is beautiful." Any man who comes to me should want to help produce a baby.

There is a difference between postponing a baby if there are serious reasons by avoiding sex at the fertile time and destroying the fertility while having sex.

Marti Armstrong: When a born-again' asks me when I became a Christian, I reply with the date of my baptism.

I get upset during the Christmas season about how Santa Claus replaces Jesus for so many people. When some of these are busy talking about what they hope Santa will bring I like to say: "Look at the word Christmas. It means Christ Mass."

Marti Armstrong relates a joke a teacher made when talking to the children at catechism about Christmas.

"So what does Christmas mean to you?" she asked. Answers included getting a doll, a train, a bicycle.

"So maybe we should call it 'Toy-Mass' instead of Christmas?"

When people blame the rise of crime on city life, I like to mutter sarcastically:

"Guess what? Cain killed Abel before industrialization!"

To understand this joke, you have to understand that while some Jesuits are leaders in the support for all Catholic teachings, others are leaders in dissent from some of these. The great Fr. John Hardon, S.J., author of *The Catechism of the Catholic Church* and a strong magisterial leader, was asked what had happened that led so many Jesuits astray. His surprising reply was said with a smile:

> "You have to understand how extremely creative Jesuits are."

During the presidential election where the Republican Candidate was John McCain and the Democratic Candidate was Obama, a priest came to an adult catechetics course wearing a vote for Obama T-shirt. I was appalled because of Obama's pro-choice platform. I asked the priest how he could consider voting for him. He replied that his family had been democratic all the way back, and he couldn't imagine voting for a man like McCain. A few weeks later in the confessional I asked:

> "So, if I kill McCain, would you vote for Sarah Palin, his running mate? And would you visit me in prison and absolve me from killing him?"

He laughed and laughed, and we were able to remain friends.

Back in the 1980's there was a big reaction to a movie made of the book *The Last Temptation of Christ* – a famous Kazantzakis novel in which Jesus has an affair with Mary Magdalene. Mother Angelica, founder of EWTN, the worldwide Catholic TV Station, was urging all her viewers to boycott the movie and protest. This went on for a few weeks. Finally, she surprised us all by stating:

> "I hope this movie dies out. I'm getting obnoxious."

On the claim there should be women priests: I say: "Suppose you were directing the Nativity Play at your parish and a famous actor happened to be in your Church. Would you choose, say, Clark Gable for the part of Mary?" So why, even a saintly woman to play the part of Jesus at the Holy Mass?

When people say the Church is so masculine, I liked to say "Oh, after Vatican II you took all the statues of the women saints and some of Mary, and then you say it's so masculine?"

When Churches were shutting because of Covid someone remarked sarcastically: "What about Wal-Mart?"

The Church teaches that Christians should live simple and austere life-styles. I interpret this to mean that I can have expensive things I need for my vocation such as a computer, or a pianist can have a piano, but not lots of stuff that is pleasurable but not needed. Especially so because others are starving whom the money for such things could feed.

Here is how I put it:

> "If you are were about to enter Wal-Mart to buy 5 Tee-shirts on sale, and you saw a starving woman in front of the door with a baby at her breast crying because she had no milk in her breast to feed it with, wouldn't you buy 1 Tee-shirt and give the rest to her?"

Oh, you might say,

"Well I don't see such people."

"But Mother Teresa's sisters feed them all over the world."

"But all these charities are questionable, there is all the overhead for managing them."

"Mother Teresa's Sisters in Calcutta, India, don't even have toilet paper, so where's the overhead?

"And, to find them, just go on search for Missionaries of Charity in the Bronx and you can send checks they will use to feed the starving."

Some Catholics nowadays do not believe in evangelizing those of other faiths on the basis that God saves everyone who is good according to the lights of their own religion. I like to say:

> "Why evangelize? If you know Jesus how can you not want everyone to know Him?"

Jokes about Vices

"I'm not an angry person, I'm just angry because everyone else is obnoxious."

"Nobody likes change, except a wet baby!" Bob Sizemore.

My godfather who was also my spiritual director once told me: "Everybody misunderstands others sometimes, but you are a genius at misunderstanding."

In anger management, a tool to repeat often to oneself through the day is this:

"Expect frustrations every five minutes, you won't be disappointed."

Alice Von Hilebrand used to teach, "The reason we hate ourselves is that we can't admire ourselves." We would like to admire ourselves as being saintly, but since we are sinners we hate ourselves, but we need, instead to humbly love ourselves as beloved repentant children of God.

In my book *The Way of Love*, I have a part called the Spiritual Marathon with programs for becoming more loving day by day. I challenge the readers in this way:

> Suppose you asked the people who know you best what they love most about you. Then ask them what defect they wish you would change.
>
> "Usually they will all agree about what is worst and you will be surprised!"
>
> Want to try?

Scruples

What are scruples? It is good to try to obey the teachings of the Church. In the case of morals, it is always obligatory. But what about the precepts of the Church? A precept is not a moral law, but the way the Church has chosen to regulate the Mass, the sacraments, and other practices. It is good to obey these, but the scrupulous person becomes obsessed with such rules in a way that drives them crazy while also being humorous. Often, the same person who is scrupulous about Catholic rules is also what is called OCD (obsessive compulsive disorder) about lots of things in life—as in alphabetizing all the herbs in the kitchen cabinet or organizing bobby-pins in rows!

Before Vatican II, Catholics would argue about whether if you bit your nails within an hour of Holy Communion, and you happened to have any food under the nails, it would be a sin.

Marti Armstrong: When I was a kid, a bad word was "bra."

Marti Armstrong: In second grade we all went to confession, and I didn't have anything to tell. So, I pretended that I ate meat on Friday. (Before Vatican II this was taught to be a sin. After that time, we were taught to do some kind of penance on Fridays, but not necessarily avoid meat.) In eighth grade, we were taught more about confession and how wrong it is to lie in confession, so I went to confession about lying in second grade about eating meat on Friday.

One Catholic dog owner wouldn't feed meat to her dog on Fridays.

I am a strong believer in living simply so that I can give lots of money to the starving all over the world through the Missionaries of Charity of Mother Teresa of Calcutta. So, I am scrupulous about buying what seem to me to be luxuries. Now, a piano isn't a luxury for a pianist, but it is when it's just for show and no one plays the piano in that house! It is perhaps overly scrupulous, though, to debate about whether Q-tips are a luxury!

My husband, however, had an opposite theory which brings a laugh to everyone I tell it to:

> "Before I was born, God set aside a whole field full of things He wanted me to enjoy. He is disappointed if I don't buy them!"

In some Catholic groups, no one uses the word cancer. They call it the big "C."

Two Catholics both wanted a cigarette while they prayed. They decided to ask a priest whether it was okay. The first asked but was told no. A little while later he spotted his friend smoking and praying. "Why did he allow you to smoke and not me?" he asked. His friend replied, "Because you asked if you could smoke while you prayed, and I asked if I could pray while I smoked!"

Elderly Jokes

I am writing this book *The Comic Catholic* when I am 85 years old (and my publisher thinks I won't remember that he waited till I was almost 88 to publish it!). I find that humor about our loss of memory and other frailties is a great help in avoiding depression about being old.

Elderly old friends mirror each other's decrepitude!

> Marti Armstrong: "If I wear these jeans to daily Mass with holes in them people will say I am holy, or they'll take up a collection and I'll be rich!"

> Bob Sizemore: "If you stopped strutting your stuff and showed your vulnerability, nurturing people would help you."

A widow friend with a large house started taking in other widows in need of the place to stay. The funny name some of us called it was "A

Homeless Shelter for Demented Catholic widows."

In old age, I have very little pressure in my fingers. As a result, I find it very hard to open jars or unscrew wine bottles. Each week there is something more I cannot easily do. To overcome an attitude of discourage despair and anger on such occasions, I like to say to myself:

> "If someone gave me $500 could I figure it out?"

It works every time!

As you grow older: "First, you don't want to leave the country. Then, you don't want to leave your city. Then, you don't want to leave your town. Then, you don't want to leave your street. Then, you don't want to leave your house. Then, you don't want to leave your bed."

When my twin-sister and I were planning a visit to the wider family that would include some nights in a hotel, I joked:

"We will sleep in the same hotel room, and we will pray ourselves back into the womb and die at the same time and have a joint funeral commemorating our illustrious lives!"

Here is how to manipulate daily Mass Catholics to do your will! Tell them you want to compose the eulogy that will get them canonized one day, but you can't unless they agree to make these changes to their lives. Of course, all changes that would benefit me!

St. John XXIII when on his death-bed called out humorously:

"My bags are packed, I'm ready to go!"

A priest became exasperated by elderly parishioners coming to see him to tell him the exact details of how they wanted him to conduct their funeral services. He claimed that the Mass itself was beautiful and that anything else they wanted should be put into the reception. He would tell us:

> "Some people are so controlling that they want to micro-manage their own funerals!"

Jesus once seemed to tell me in prayer for my old age: "Don't dog-paddle in the waves of life. Let me float you to the shore."

Jokes about Heaven and Hell

I think that there are so many jokes about heaven and hell because most Catholics, no matter how faithful, are afraid of hell. Here are some I especially enjoy:

> "A man is ushered past the gates of heaven into a room. He sits down at the table and is offered bread and water. He looks down through the floor and sees hell with everyone eating good food. He complains to his attendant. 'Why is it that they in hell are eating delicious food and I only get bread and water?'"
>
> The reply is: "It's harder to cook for one."

When Christians are discouraged by world events some preachers tell them: "Read the end of the book: we win!"

My friend, Bill Cotter, Director of Operation Rescue in Boston, had a bumper sticker that said,

"For eternal life, do you prefer smoking or non-smoking."

My friend, Mike Bourque, a member of the Boston Street preachers, whenever anybody asked him where he's going, would say, "Heaven, I hope."

A person goes to Confession and says, "But I was not the only one concerning that bad deed." The priest said, "That is the consolation in hell: I'm not the only one."

When visiting family for long periods of time, I hate to see food getting wasted and thrown out. Since cooking vegetable soup is one of my only culinary successes, I put everything that would go into the trash eventually into the soup and call it jokingly "Garbage Soup." One of my grandchildren was talking to his friends about what hell would be like. He offered this definition:

> "Hell is having to eat my Grandma's garbage soup."

Old Gospel Song: “If I get to heaven before you do, I’ll dig a little hole and pull you through.”

I like to say: “If anyone who tries so much as I do to be good doesn’t get into purgatory, who will?”

Jokes that Seem to Indicate God's Sense of Humor

Is God ever humorous? You might think not. But Thomas Aquinas taught that everything is received according to the nature of the recipient. So, I think it is possible that if God made me to have such a strong sense of humor, He could sometimes joke with me, such as in these instances.

I had spent a lot of money to travel to Rome for a special audience with John Paul II. The editor of a book of writings by professors about his ideas would be presented to him. I thought this would be my great, great father-healing when JPII looks into my eyes with love. I kept thinking there would be some obstacle, but there we were, the writers, walking up to his chair, surrounding him and one by one talking to him for a few moments. About a third of us had gone up and gotten the blessing. But, then, the Swiss Guards came up and announced: "The Holy Father isn't feeling well. There are too many people around him." Then they led the rest of us away.

We were celebrating at a restaurant after the event. Sitting on the toilet at the restaurant, I was crying. "The others got the blessing, but not me!" It seemed to me that St. Catherine of Siena told me with words in my heart: "Ronda, you become a saint, and people will be begging for your autograph!"

Jesus seemed to tell me once: "Ronda, if you become a saint, your books will sell better!"

Jesus, also, once seemed to tell me:

> "Ronda, stop scheming to avoid suffering."

A well-known charismatic healing priest of an Italian ancestry liked to make meatballs and spaghetti after the Sunday Masses. A woman came to the rectory in a wild state about her husband's having a terrible fear of death that seemed imminent. He had received the anointing of the sick, but couldn't this priest also come and be with him? The priest put some meatballs in a plastic container and said, "Give him these." She took them and returned to say her husband was completely healed after eating them!

St. Joseph Cupertino who couldn't learn Latin well enough but became a priest in spite of this, used to be seen levitated on the ceiling of the Church.

I was enjoying immensely Tchaikovsky's 1st Piano Concerto. I asked Jesus if He liked it. He seemed to reply: "Who do you think inspired him to compose it?"

I am terrible at physical pain…Jesus seemed to tell me once:

> "You would like to have dramatic physical pain in union with Me, such as the stigmata. I give you very little physical pain because you are such a wimp. It is better to give you emotional pain."

I was trying to remember the next morning how many decades of the rosary I had said before falling asleep. Jesus seemed to joke:

"So, now you're a mathematician?"

Angels are not Gods, but they are still supernatural beings. Once I asked my Guardian Angel:

"How can you stand living with me?"

"It's a challenge!" he seemed to quip.

Since I am very pushy, always trying to get Catholics to be involved in my projects. Jesus seemed to tell me: "Don't push, respond!"

Jokes from my Life and Family

This chapter has jokes that are funny for me and my family in a personal way, but I notice when I tell these stories everyone laughs. So, you are welcome to see what you think.

When I was a girl of about 9 years old, living in a neighborhood just like in the movie West Side Story, I was coming home from school when 3 or 4 gang kids, Irish Catholics, surrounded me and my sister:

"Are you a Catholic?"
"No."
"Are you a Protestant?
"No."
"Are you Jewish?"
"No." (At that time I didn't know we were Jewish because my atheist parents didn't believe in religious background as part of one's identity)
"So, what are you?"

"Atheists."

Since they didn't know what an atheist was, they let us go.

When I first started teaching full-time at a Catholic university, back in 1969, I had a group of students who loved my classes. They used to have gatherings at one of their houses. They invited me. How sad, I thought that they are so poor they can't even buy a package of cigarettes. I told them how sorry I was for them. They laughed and laughed. They were passing around a marijuana joint. I had never seen one before!

I used to have my twins put all their toys in their beds while singing "The Saints Go Marching In."

My son, Charlie, said some very funny things as a boy. In school they told the students to write a one line description of each of their parents.

"My mom is a small fierce philosopher," Charlie wrote.

I was feeling low one day. I almost never went to what was then called a beauty parlor because I like to avoid luxuries and give the money to the starving. But one day in my late forties I felt depressed and decided to try getting a perm. I came home with my long straight hair now short and curly.

"For other women it's okay, Mom," said my 8-year-old son, "but for you it's a sin."

When my daughter, Diana, was twelve, she was in a craft class in school. They had them make a business card for someone. She asked me if she could make one for me. Here is what she put on it:

> "Ronda Chervin, Ph.D.: part time saint, full time martyr!

When my daughters were teens, they sometimes hung out in front of the 7/11 store and chatted with young men. On the way home, they realized a group of these were chasing after them.

They got in the front door, and we locked that and the back door and since they wouldn't leave, we called the police. In Los Angeles, even back then, there was so much crime that the police didn't come right away for calls such as ours. Looking out the back windows we saw the young men, probably on drugs, were hiding in the bushes. Finally, we heard the police siren. Diana ran to the back door and warned them to get away. They did. Afterwards, I asked Diana why she had done this, preventing the police from arresting them:

"Mom, what would St. Francis have done?"

When, as a philosophy professor and writer, I became a Catholic speaker, often after a talk a woman would come up and begin her question with this apology: "I'm just a housewife, but…?"

I would ask: "How many children do you have?"

At the answer usually of 5 or 6 I would put it this humorous way:

"Well, I had 3 children and 4 miscarriages. Which of your children do you wish you hadn't had so you could have written a book in your spare time?... A book that will one day be in the incinerator while that child will live for all eternity!"

After my husband died, I decided to try becoming a Dedicated Widow. This involves making a private promise not to re-marry and having a rule of life approved by a priest. In my case, I wanted to wear a simple blue jumper and white or blue blouse and a blue kerchief around my head. I was visiting Diana and asked her to come with me to the store. She said: "No. I will not go with you. I do not want to look like the illegitimate child of a monk-ess."

A reason to be careful about marrying a woman philosopher is that some of us are such air-heads that it is hard for us to pay attention to practical details of life. A few examples: I would start cooking burgers in the frying pan, get an idea for an essay I was writing, leave the stove and come back to find the burgers were tough as bullets. I figure my guardian angel drove my car most of the time. Was he taking a nap when I had my few accidents?

One of our funniest family stories is this one: Just after my husband died, when we had been living in a large house in Southern California with my daughter, son-in-law, and children, the famous Northridge earthquake hit. We were just in the process of getting an equity loan. The company called and insisted we immediately sign the documents because our house would lose value up to $100,000 because of damage from the quake. We drove across three freeways, avoiding the security police who wanted no one to drive in case of a second quake! I moved to another state alone. Five years later, I got a letter from that loan company to this effect:

> "We have been looking for you because you owe us $50,000. But we are also looking for your daughter and her husband. If you give us their contact information we will waive your debt."

I immediately called my daughter: "I won't turn you in, but....!!!!! What shall I do?"

She laughed loudly and replied: "April fool!"

Once I was in a car crash. I was in the front seat, but not the driver. In those days I wore a prothesis, a false cotton breast, in place of the flat surface where one of my breasts had been removed because of cancer. I took it off on long drives since it was uncomfortable. None of us in the car was hurt, but since the car was totaled, the fire department came and took us to the hospital for x-rays to be sure. As they led me to their vehicle one of them told me:

"Since the car is totaled and you may never see it again, do you have anything valuable in the car we can take out now?"

"Hmmmm. Oh, yes, I left my breast in front of my seat."

He was surprised. I laughed and laughed.

At the last class I taught before retiring, I quipped:

"You are the last people in the whole world who will ever obey me!"

Gary McCabe, a wonderful Catholic evangelist, when asked to be part of "perfect" newly forming communities likes to quip: "Every utopia becomes a gulag."

I entitled one of my last books *Nine Toes in Eternity*.

Last Joke?

I instructed one of the Catholic members of my family to arrange this for my funeral:

> Put in the casket a tape-recorder. After the last blessings before they roll to coffin out of the Church, someone hits the button, and everyone hears me say:
>
> "You knew I would try to get in the last word, didn't you? So, everyone here I have ever hurt, please forgive me. And, if you love me anyhow and want to see me again, there are quite a few priests here. Go to confession and be a good Christian and one day we will all be together forever in heaven."

Guess what? So far, I can't get a priest to agree to this "innovation."

www.ingramcontent.com/pod-product-compliance
Lightning Source LLC
LaVergne TN
LVHW040223110826
845146LV00004B/1272